OCT   2002

WIT

D1084829

The Little Dipper

Stephanie True Peters

The Rosen Publishing Group
PowerKids Press
New York

For Mom, who always said I was born under a lucky star

Published in 2003 by The Rosen Publishing Group, Inc.
29 East 21st Street, New York, NY 10010
Copyright © 2003 by The Rosen Publishing Group, Inc.

First Edition
Editors: Gillian Houghton, Jannell Khu
Book Design: Michael Caroleo, Michael Donnellan, Michael de Guzman
Photo Credits: cover, pp. 4, 16 © Roger Ressmeyer/CORBIS; title page, p. 12, back cover (constellation) Bode's Uranographia, 1801, courtesy of the Science, Industry & Business Library, the New York Public Library, Astor, Lenox and Tilden Foundations; pp. 6, 7 © Stapleton Collection/CORBIS; pp. 8, 10, 15 digital illustration by Michael de Guzman; p. 11 © KymThalassoudis; p. 12 (man with sextant) © Bettmann/CORBIS; p. 19 digital illustration by Michael Caroleo; p. 20 courtesy of NASA/JPL/California Institute of Technology.

Peters, Stephanie True, 1965–
The Little Dipper / Stephanie True Peters.— 1st ed.
    p. cm.
Includes bibliographical references and index.
Summary: Describes the constellation known as the Little Dipper.
  ISBN 0-8239-6163-X (library binding)
1. Ursa Minor (Constellation)—Juvenile literature. [1. Ursa Minor (Constellation)] I. Title.
QB802 .P43 2003
  523.8—dc21

                                                                                    2001004455

Manufactured in the United States of America

Contents

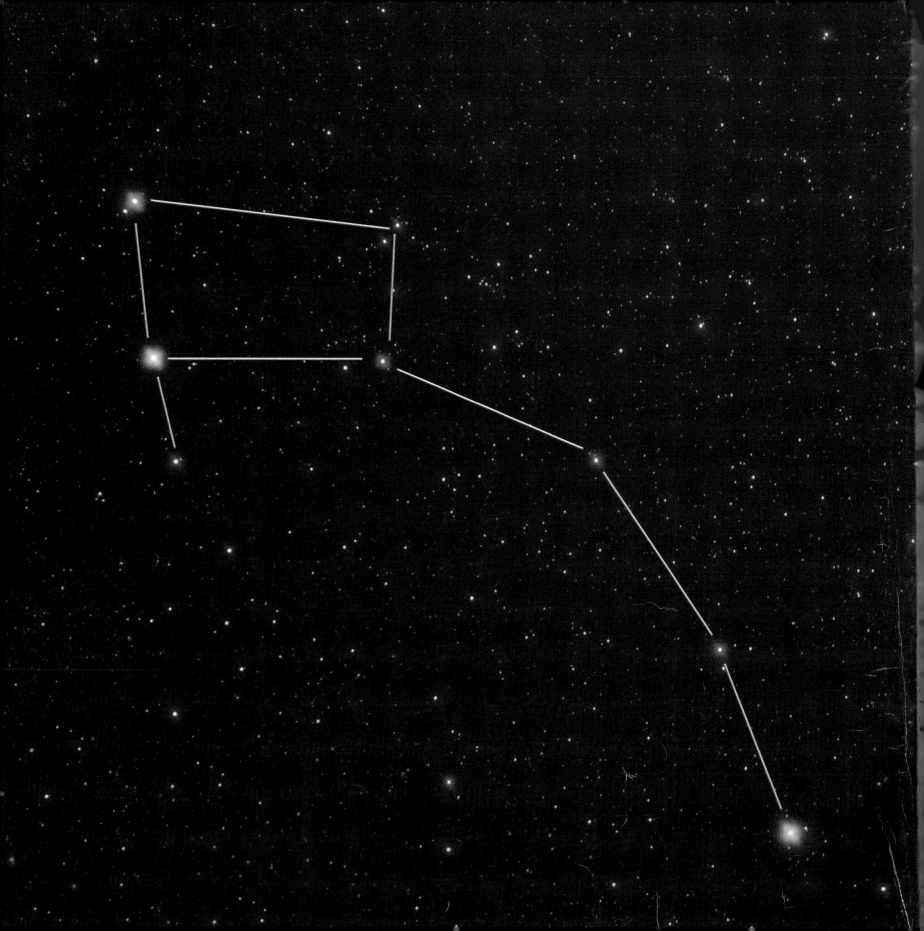

The Little Dipper

When you gaze at the night sky, one of the easiest star groups to find is the Big Dipper. Trace a line through the outer stars of the Big Dipper's bowl, and you will find **Polaris**, the North Star. Once you find Polaris, you should be able to find the other dipper in the sky, the Little Dipper. The Little Dipper is made up of seven stars. Four stars outline its small bowl. Three stars form the handle. Polaris is the last star in the Little Dipper's handle. The Little Dipper is not a true constellation, which is a formation of stars that has been given a name. The Little Dipper is an asterism, a group of stars that is part of a larger constellation.

Fun Facts

When you look up into the night sky, it almost looks as if the stars are close together. However, they are far apart from one another. Some stars that appear to be close to one another are hundreds of thousands of miles apart!

Polaris is the bright star at the tip of the Little Dipper's handle.

Arcas, the Little Bear

The Little Dipper is part of a constellation known as **Ursa Minor**, or the Little Bear. The ancient Greeks had many **myths** about how the Little Bear came to be. One story told how Zeus, the king of the gods, fell in love with a **nymph** named Callisto. They had a son together and named him Arcas. When Zeus's wife, Hera, found out, she was angry. Hera turned Callisto into a bear.

Many men, including Arcas, hunted the bear. Arcas did not know the bear was his mother. To save Callisto from her son's arrow, Zeus turned her into the constellation Ursa Major, or the Great Bear. Zeus pulled Arcas into the sky, too, and turned him into the group of stars called the Little Bear.

According to an ancient Greek story, when Zeus pulled Arcas into the sky, he stretched Arcas's tail. That is why the Little Bear has such a long tail!

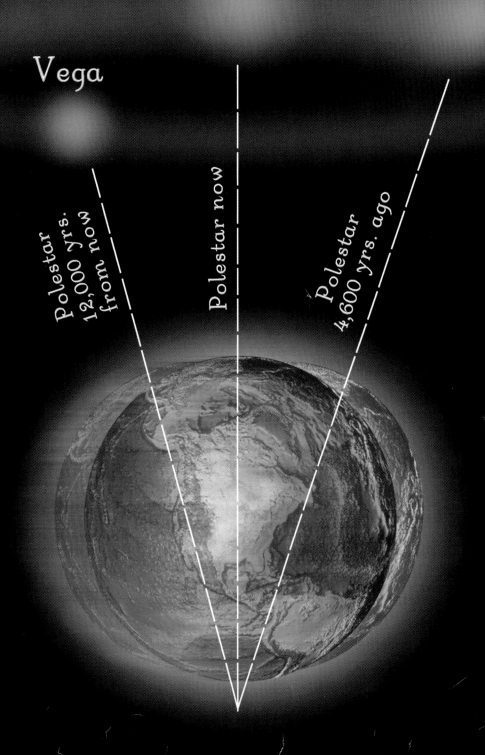

Polaris

Thuban

Vega

Polestar 12,000 yrs. from now

Polestar now

Polestar 4,600 yrs. ago

Polaris, the Polestar

Polaris is an important star, because it sits above the North Pole. For that reason, Polaris is also called the polestar. This important star was not always the polestar, and it will not be the polestar forever.

A star named Thuban was the polestar 4,600 years ago. **Astronomers** think that in 12,000 years a star known as Vega will become the polestar. The polestar changes because Earth wobbles, like a spinning top, as it turns on its **axis**. Today the handle of the Little Dipper points to Polaris. Through the course of thousands of years, the handle will point toward a different star.

Fun Facts

There is a Paiute Native American story about a mountain sheep named Na-Gah who became the North Star. Na-Gah always climbed to reach the highest mountain peak. When he finally reached it, the Paiute god Shinob rewarded Na-Gah's bravery and turned him into the North Star.

Polaris will not be the polestar forever. Thuban was the polestar 4,600 years ago, and Vega will be the polestar 12,000 years from now.

Mapping the Sky

For centuries people have recognized Ursa Minor and its famous asterism, the Little Dipper. Ancient Egyptian and ancient Greek astronomers charted Ursa Minor and 47 other constellations. Today we know that there are 88 official constellations. If there are 88 constellations, why did ancient people chart only 48? When you look up at the sky, you can see only part of the universe that surrounds Earth. The rest is hidden from view behind the **horizon**. The ancient Egyptian and ancient Greek astronomers, who first mapped the constellations, lived in the Northern **Hemisphere**. They could see only the 48 constellations that were visible in the northern sky. Later when people first traveled below the **equator**, they realized that there were many more star groups in the sky. Most of the 40 constellations unseen by early astronomers can be seen only from the Southern Hemisphere.

This star chart shows the stars of the Northern Hemisphere as they appear in winter. Ursa Major (circled and inset) is visible in the Northern Hemisphere.

CAUDA DRACONIS

URSA MINOR

CAMELOPARDALUS

Star Calendars, Star Maps

For centuries the stars have helped people to figure out what season it was. This lets people know when to farm and when to harvest. Before calendars were invented, the stars helped farmers in mild climates keep track of the different seasons. Some constellations can be seen only during certain seasons. Farmers knew that when springtime constellations were in the sky, it was time to plant crops. When fall constellations appeared in the sky, it was time to harvest.

Stars also have been used as maps to help people find their way. Travelers have used the stars to **navigate** on land and at sea. Polaris, the tip of the Little Dipper's handle, is also known as the North Star. A sailor or an explorer who moved toward the North Star knew he was traveling north. He knew that west was to the left, east was to the right, and that the south was behind him. When he measured how far Polaris appeared above the horizon, he could also figure out how far above the equator he was.

For centuries explorers used instruments such as sextants to navigate. A sextant establishes the distance of a star, such as Polaris, from the horizon.

Where to Find the Little Dipper

The Little Dipper can be seen faintly year-round. Each day it rises in the East and sets in the West, like the Sun. Throughout the year, the Little Dipper slowly circles around Polaris counterclockwise. Each season, it is in a different position. Face north as you look at the night sky. Imagine the Little Dipper as a bowl with a long handle. In the winter, the bowl of the Little Dipper looks like it is resting upright on a table. In the spring, it appears to be balanced on its handle. The Little Dipper is upside down throughout the summer. In the fall, its handle points up, and the bowl is balanced on its side.

Fun Facts

In the Northern Hemisphere, the constellations appear to circle the polestar each year. In the Southern Hemisphere, the constellations appear to circle the South Pole. For centuries navigators found the South Pole with the help of the constellation Crux, the Southern Cross.

If you face north in the Northern Hemisphere and observe the stars each season, you will see the Little Dipper and the Big Dipper as they are shown here.

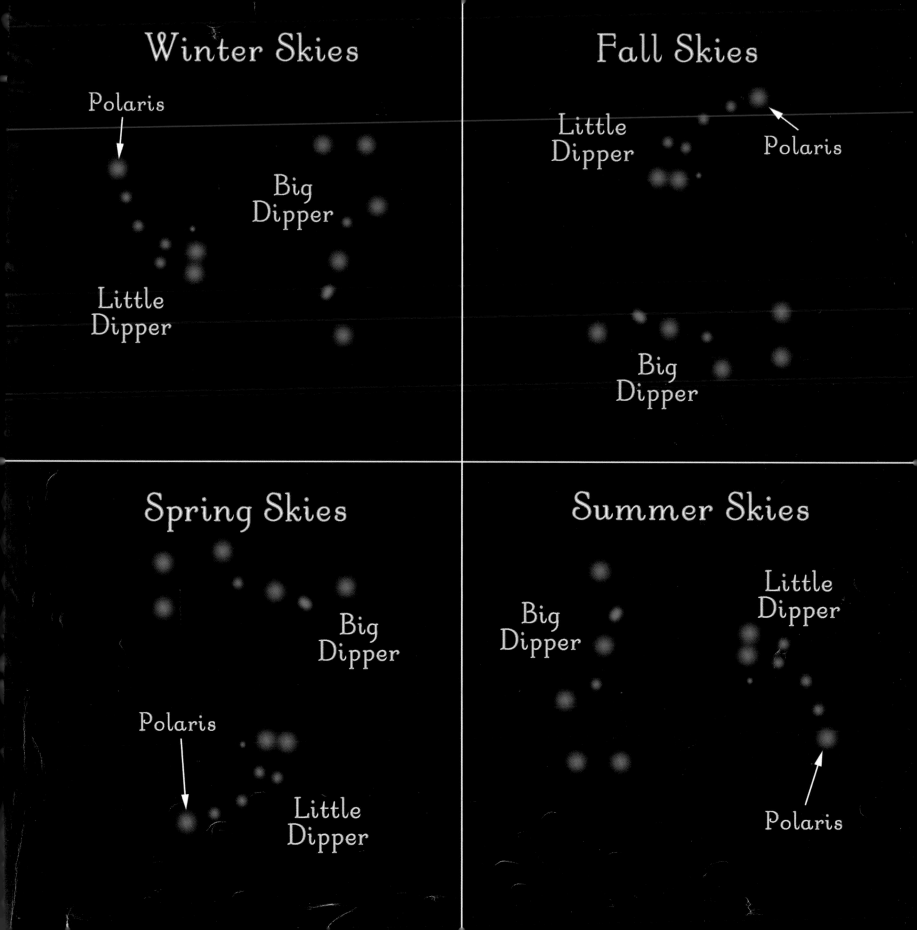

North Star / Polaris

Magnitude: 1.97

Magnitude

Even if you know where to look, the Little Dipper can be difficult to see unless the night sky is very clear. This is because most of the stars that form the Little Dipper are faint. We describe how bright a star is by its **magnitude**. Magnitude is a scale of measurement. The higher the number is on the scale, the fainter the star. Stars that have a magnitude of 1, or stars of the first magnitude, are very bright. Stars of the sixth magnitude are the faintest stars we can see without binoculars or a telescope. Polaris is the brightest star in the Little Dipper. It has a magnitude of almost 2. The faintest star in the Little Dipper has a magnitude of 5. If you can see all the stars in the Little Dipper, it is either a great night for stargazing, or you have very good eyesight!

Polaris, the brightest star in the Little Dipper, has a magnitude of 2. On star maps, bright stars are represented as large dots, and dim stars are represented as small dots.

Twinkle, Twinkle

When you look at a star in the Little Dipper, you might think it is **flickering**. Its brightness appears to change, but it does not. To understand why, imagine that you are at a pool. You dive in and open your eyes under the water to see a friend sitting on the pool's edge. Even if the water is calm, your friend looks unclear and seems to move. Your friend has not changed, however. The water makes it difficult to see your friend clearly.

Something like this happens when you look up at the night sky. A layer of air that is nearly 600 miles (966 km) deep surrounds Earth. This air, called the **atmosphere**, acts as the pool water does in the example. You have to look through hundreds of miles of atmosphere to see the stars. The air, filled with dust and pollution, makes the stars appear to twinkle. This twinkling is called **stellar scintillation**.

The atmosphere, the layer of air surrounding Earth, is made up of dust, water vapor, and gases that include nitrogen and oxygen.

Space Telescopes

Astronomers have special instruments that help them to see the stars more clearly. They launch space telescopes into **orbit** around Earth. The telescopes circle Earth above the atmosphere, the layer of air that blurs our view of the stars. The space telescope travels above the atmosphere and views the stars clearly.

The Hubble Space Telescope is a famous and powerful telescope. It was named after an American astronomer, Edwin Powell Hubble, and was launched on April 24, 1990. The telescope is about the size of a school bus and weighs 12 tons (11 t)! It travels at 5 miles per second (8 km/sec) and completes one trip around Earth in just 97 minutes. Astronomers control the telescope from Earth, and every day they take enough pictures to fill an encyclopedia. The pictures they take are the clearest images of the stars people ever have seen.

The Hubble Space Telescope travels 380 miles (612 km) above Earth's surface, where temperatures range from -250°F to 100°F (-157°C–37°C).

Planetariums

You can learn more about the stars on the Internet and at your library. You also can visit a **planetarium**. A planetarium is like a movie theater. The domed ceiling serves as the screen. A special **projector** in the middle of the theater flashes images of the night sky on the ceiling. A narrator explains what the images are. If you visit a planetarium, you will probably see the Little Dipper projected on the ceiling and will hear the story of Callisto and her son, Arcas. Many planetariums are also museums that show rare books and astronomical instruments, such as **astrolabes**, and explain the history of astronomy.

Fun Facts

Polaris is also known as the lodestar. Lodestone is a naturally-occurring rock used to make compasses. Compasses are instruments that use Earth's magnetic pull to establish direction. Like the lodestone, Polaris can direct lost travelers to the correct path.

Glossary

astrolabes (AS-truh-laybz) Instruments that measure the positions of stars, used to navigate the oceans.

astronomers (uh-STRAH-nuh-merz) People who study the Sun, the Moon, the planets, and the stars.

atmosphere (AT-muh-sfeer) The layer of gases that surrounds an object in space. On Earth, this layer is air.

axis (AK-sis) A straight line on which an object turns or seems to turn.

equator (ih-KWAY-tur) An imaginary line around Earth that separates it into two parts, northern and southern.

flickering (FLIH-ker-ing) Burning with an unsteady light.

hemisphere (HEH-muh-sfeer) Half of a sphere or globe.

horizon (her-EYE-zun) A line where the sky seems to meet Earth.

launch (LAWNCH) When a spacecraft is pushed into the air.

magnitude (MAG-nih-tood) The measurement of a star's brightness.

myths (MITHS) Stories that people make up to explain events.

navigate (NA-vuh-gayt) To explore.

nymph (NIHMF) A beautiful maiden who lives in the forests, trees, and water in Greek myths.

orbit (OR-bit) The circular path traveled by planets and other objects in space around a fixed object.

planetarium (pla-nih-TAYR-ee-um) A theater with a domed ceiling used for looking at images of the night sky.

Polaris (poh-LAR-us) The North Star, or polestar.

projector (pruh-JEK-ter) An instrument that causes light, shadow, or images to fall on a surface.

stellar scintillation (STEH-lur sin-til-AY-shun) The twinkling of stars.

Ursa Minor (ER-suh MY-ner) The constellation that includes the polestar and the stars that form the Big Dipper.

Index

Web Sites

To learn more about constellations and the Little Dipper, check out these Web sites:
http://einstein.stcloudstate.edu/Dome/constellns/umi.html
www.enchantedlearning.com/subjects/astronomy